all-nighter**writer**™

ALL-NIGHTER WRITER / CAMBRIDGE MA
THE ARCHITECT PAINTER PRESS / BOSTON MA

all-nighter writer™

END YOUR WRITING NIGHTMARES

volume **1**

Marilyn JONES PhD

This book sticks to four simple goals. Advertising guru Leo Burnett explains them best:

"Make it simple.

Make it memorable.

Make it inviting to look at.

Make it fun to read."

All-Nighter Writer:
END YOUR WRITING NIGHTMARES
Volume 1

All-Nighter Writer
63 MOUNT VERNON STREET | SUITE 1
CAMBRIDGE, MA 02140

THE ARCHITECT PAINTER PRESS
ASTOR STATION | PO BOX 230952
BOSTON, MA 02123-0952

All photos by Marilyn Jones or Eliot Plum.

www.allnighterwriter.com

Email: **contact@allnighterwriter.com**
a. Report glitches
b. Ask questions
c. Sign up for workshops or one-on-one coaching
d. Thunder and shout

Endless thanks to my terrific support team—Rebecca Toedter, Seth Toedter, Alex Roth, Karim Ajania, and The Architect Painter Press. I couldn't have done this project without you. Especially you, Eliot Plum. And my deepest gratitude to Joan Stockbridge, who began this writing and teaching journey with me 20 years ago. Our professional relationship during those early years together—and our abiding friendship—means more than words can say.

contents

End your writemares and change how you write—overnight.

introduction

YOU—THE PERSON LOOKING AT THIS BOOK!

All-Nighter Writer knows who you are (and you're not alone):
You have to write—and you need help.

All-Nighter Writer to the rescue!

Look around: You live in a Web-based, image-driven culture. Yet you labor under 20th-century rules and forms of writing that you either never learned, can't remember, or just don't understand.

All-Nighter Writer can help.

 ANW doesn't teach fuzzy, confusing rules.

 ANW doesn't teach highfalutin language.

ANW *does* teach the logic and principles of English so people can write in the real world.

As an editor, I see the traps people fall into as they try to express themselves. As a former university teacher, I know only too well the abyss that most students face when trying to write. And as the parent of children who have graduated from private colleges, I know that even the best education money can buy doesn't guarantee that students will learn to write.

What to do?
I've taken matters into my own hands.

Buckle up, my friends:
You're about to learn to write.

The first draft of anything is %#@!. [Ernest Hemingway

If you don't know

where you're going,
you'll end up somewhere else.

gpsforyour

document

Plan your trip.

1

THINK OF PLANNING A TRIP.

YOU PROBABLY DO THE FOLLOWING:

- Decide on your destination
- Pack appropriately
- Leave good stuff behind for another trip
- Travel light
- Take a map
- Follow directions

SO DO SMART WRITERS.

Before you write a single word, draw a map of your article.

First draw a bubble . . . .

Call this

Step 1:
ACTION MEMO TO SELF

Inside the bubble include the following:

- An action verb (persuade/convince/request/analyze/summarize/inspire)
- Your audience
- What you want to convey

Example:

Persuade reader
capital punishment
is wrong.

This directive to yourself will guide you from start to finish as you write your article. You will ask yourself with each sentence, with each point you make: "Does this help persuade my reader that capital punishment is wrong?" If not, change your sentence or leave it out. And continue to follow your map.

Call this

Step 2:
MINDSTORMING

Take five minutes or less to decide on categories. These might include the following: opening, conclusion, data, opposing point of view, history of problem, supporting quotes.

Each of these categories gets its own bubble, and you "mindstorm" under each category as exhaustively as you can before you move to the next category's bubble. Do one bubble at a time.

Once you've done this mindstorming, you can start your article. Once you've begun, decide as you go when to introduce the information in the various bubbles. Unlike traditional outlines, your mindmap doesn't depend on a hierarchy of ideas. **You** decide when to introduce each section—each "bubble." Some choices will stand out as obvious: **introduction, conclusion, opposing point of view** (should go close to the opening). But you decide how to best organize the structure of your document.

Once you have your GPS in front of you, you will have the freedom to concentrate on the quality of your writing, secure in knowing that you have already decided what to include and what not to include.

This GPS map will relieve you of 50% of writing stress and 50% of the rewriting required to polish the next draft. You won't have to rewrite to include the points you meant to make or delete the points you later realize detract from your overall thesis.

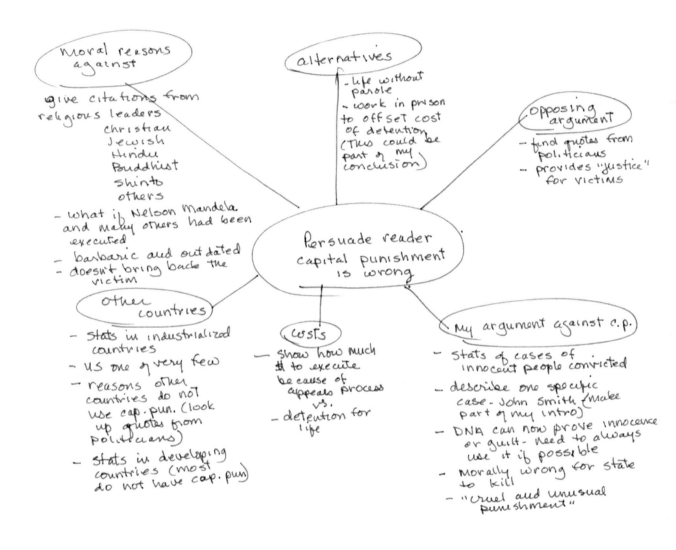

GPS EXAMPLE

GPS YOUR DOCUMENT

AND NEVER GET LOST.

You don't get a second chance to make a first impression.

at hello

Open with a hook.

THE FIRST JOB OF THE WRITER?

GET YOUR READER'S ATTENTION.

And once you've gotten your reader's attention, you have to keep your reader with you.

You have to do the work.

Why? Because your reader doesn't have to read your article, essay, letter, or email. Your reader has countless other articles, essays, letters, and emails to read. Along with blogs, websites, reviews, editorials, text messages, Tweets, Facebook, and Japanese anime comic books.

Okay—a few exceptions:
- Your professor probably has to read your paper.
- You have to read some tedious chapter because you will have a test on it next Tuesday.

Otherwise, writers face a lot of competition. Look at Madison Avenue: Billions of dollars every year go to finding that one line, that tag, those few words that will crack through the avalanche of ads and verbiage to hit home. And stick.

"Just do it." (Nike)

"Drivers wanted." (Volkswagen)

"Nothing runs like a Deere." (Deere Tractors)

"You're in good hands." (Allstate Insurance)

Or the unforgettable movie lines. We know them, even if we haven't seen the movies:

"Make my day." (*Dirty Harry*)

"Show me the money." (*Jerry McGuire*)

"Beam me up, Scotty." (*Star Trek*)

REMEMBER: Flat, boring first lines signal flat, boring writing. Nobody wants to go there.

31

Let's look at some flat openings:

1. BEFORE: In J.D. Salinger's controversial 1951 novel *The Catcher in the Rye*, the main character is Holden Caulfield.

AFTER: I am Holden Caulfield. I'll bet a lot of people have said that after they've read J.D. Salinger's *Catcher in the Rye*.

2. BEFORE: James Baldwin was the author of many works such as *Giovanni's Room*, *Another Country*, and *The Fire Next Time*. As a young boy in Harlem, his talent with words was seen.

AFTER: During the 1930's, young James Baldwin, poor and living in Harlem, made it into a prestigious high school in the Bronx because he had something he couldn't hide: talent.

3. BEFORE: This essay will compare and contrast the protagonist/ antagonist's relationship with each other and the other jurors in the play and in the movie versions of Reginald Rose's *12 Angry Men*.

AFTER: Everybody expected the defendant would hang—until one lone juror had the audacity to vote "not guilty" on the first ballet.

4. BEFORE: The story "A Clean, Well-Lighted Place" is written by Ernest Hemingway. In this story he shows the difference between the light and darkness.

AFTER: Hemingway knows how you feel. How anyone feels out there in the dark.

The "after" examples hook the reader's interest. Later in the essay, the writer can naturally insert the information that we see crammed into the "before" examples.

So how do you hook your reader?

First lines can do it.

Let's look at some great openings.
See how they do at least one of the following:

- Prompt you to keep going
- Pose a question you just have to have answered
- Intrigue you with an interesting voice
- Promise an original world you want to enter
- Provide specific details that pique your interest

1. " 'Finding an apartment is a lot like falling in love,' the real-estate agent told us. She was a stylish grandmother in severe designer sunglasses." (David Sedaris—*The New Yorker*) [intriguing voice; a new world]

2. "One July morning last year in Oklahoma City, in a public-housing project named Sooner Haven, twenty-two-year-old Kim Henderson pulled a pair of low-rider jeans over a high-rising gold lamé thong and declared herself ready for church." (Katherine Boo, "The Marriage Cure"—*The New Yorker*) [intriguing voice; a new world]

3. "Five minutes before we boarded the plane to Africa, Al Sharpton called the group into a circle to pray. It struck me as a fine idea." (Tucker Carlson, "The League of Extraordinary Gentlemen"—*Esquire*) [intriguing voice; poses questions]

4. "In Rwanda, evil has a name, an address, and a bunk bed." ("Healing Genocide"—*Christianity Today*) [intriguing voice; a new world]

5. "The sandstorms blowing through Iraq left a kind of mustard cloud over the desert flats of Qatar, creating a fair approximation of the end of the earth. Serendipitously, 'Midnight at the Oasis' was playing on the car radio as I came up to the camp gate just before 5 a.m.—my tenth day in Doha." (Michael Wolff, "My Big Fat Question"—*New York Magazine*) [intriguing voice; a new world]

6. "We were in Linc's car, an aging yellow Mercedes sedan, big and steady, with slippery blond seats and a deep, strumming idle. Lincoln called it Dr. Diesel. It was a Sunday night, March 22, 1987, nine-thirty. Rural Ohio was a smooth continuity of silence and darkness, except for a faintly golden seam where land met sky ahead, promising light and people and sound just beyond the tree line." (Laura Hillenbrand, "A Sudden Illness" —*The New Yorker*) [intriguing voice; a new world; poses questions]

7. "Lugging backpacks and Hefty bags on Sunday at sunrise, they trickle in to the expanse of dirt and gravel under Interstate 35. Littering this city block between 4th and 5th streets in Waco, Texas are taillight shards, pigeon feathers, and at least one dead bat. The men sit mostly in solitude at the base of support columns, waiting for something to happen." (Deann Alford, "A Bridge Over Troubled People," *Christianity Today*) [a new world; poses questions]

Tricks of the GREAT OPENING:

You can find several ways to get started. If you struggle with the opening, let it go and come back to it after you've written your article or essay.

But if you get your opening rolling, you will find yourself blasting right on through until you reach the conclusion. (We'll talk about how—and how not—to end later.)

You can start *in media res*—Latin for "into mid-affairs." Which refers to a literary and artistic technique where the narrative starts in the middle of the action. You then backtrack to fill in the backstory.

Look at examples 1, 4, and 7 on pages 33 and 34. In each of these examples, the writer drops the reader cinematically right into the scene.

- We want to know more.
- We want to know more about these people.
- We want to know *why*—we want our questions answered.

"Read on, dear reader," these first lines say, "because I've hooked you!"

Paint an original, intriguing world.

Look at all of the examples that start *in media res*. The writer brings us into a world we haven't seen before.

We want to see more of this world.

Create a voice so intriguing and original that your reader must get to know you and see the world through your unique point of view.

In the other examples, the quirky, off-kilter voice of the writer intrigues us and promises:
"You'll see life from a new perspective, so stay with me."

Although, What, Because

If you feel so stuck at the outset that you can't find a way to open an essay or article, you can rely on this strategy. When I was in the PhD program at the University of California, Davis, my fellow graduate student Kevin Clark taught me this sure-fire strategy:

Kevin called this the "Although, what, because" opening.

Once you get this in your arsenal, you can start any written exam, or any paper or article, and you will not only get your opening taken care of, you can use this opening to structure your entire essay.

Let's use a hypothetical essay topic.

You have to write on capital punishment. Let's say you're against it. (This works just as well if you're for it. The point here: Take a position and argue for it.)

1. Opposing point of view—the "although"
Start with the "although" part of your argument (which you have to address in any good piece of writing).

Before you launch into your good reasons for doing away with capital punishment, you must address the opposing side of the argument. You show you have considered the whole question and you can understand that some points could sway someone to the opposite point of view. Here we have the "although" part of the argument:

Open with a hook.

"Although many people believe that capital punishment serves as an effective deterrent to crime and keeps society stable and carries out justice, ..."

You've shown that you know others have valid points to make.

2. You will now show that you take a different point of view—the "<u>what</u>" of your argument:

"I'm against capital punishment because it undermines the fairness and forward progress of society . . . . "

3. And now for the meat of your essay—the "<u>because</u>":

" . . . because studies show that capital punishment has no effect whatsoever on crime statistics, because all other developed countries around the world have banned capital punishment because of its cruel, barbarian nature, and because capital punishment undermines the integrity and moral stature of a nation."

Now this looks like a long, unwieldy opening sentence, which it is. Break it up, and make it a short paragraph. Make it three paragraphs. Trim or expand as you see fit.

But follow the principle:

Although (the opposing viewpoint), **what** (your point of view), **because** (the reasons that support your point of view).

You can now organize your entire article or essay on this structure. Remember to keep your "although" section in one unit, your "because" statement or statements in one unit, and your "because" part of the essay in one unit. You'll have transitions between the sections, but don't mix up the three units.

ALTHOUGH: First, write one, two, or three sentences or paragraphs or three pages—to focus on and expand the "although."

WHAT: Write a short paragraph to link your fundamental point—"I don't agree with capital punishment."

BECAUSE: And then take 10 paragraphs or 20 pages to support and explain your very good reasons—your "because."

THESIS STATEMENT

If you've ever taken an English class, you've heard this scary term: "thesis statement."

Relax. It just sounds complicated and fuzzy. Actually, all you need to do?

State your **point of view** on the topic you're writing about. Ask yourself:

- Why would my reader want to read this essay?
- What significant point am I going to make?
- And how will I persuade my reader to agree with my point of view?

A thesis statement tells the reader **your point of view on a subject**—not simply the subject itself: Reader alert! Get ready to find out **why** i wrote about this topic!

You'll want to get this **Reader Alert** into the beginning of the essay—ideally, in the first paragraph.

EXAMPLE:

BEFORE:
Nathaniel Hawthorne wrote *The Scarlet Letter*, a novel about cultural and religious intolerance in 17th-century Boston.
(The sentence states the subject itself—not your interpretation or point of view.)

AFTER:

In his novel *The Scarlet Letter*, Nathaniel Hawthorne used contrasting images of wild forests and staid, suffocating town life as metaphors to show the unconscionable religious hypocrisy of 17th-century Boston.
(The reader has a reason to keep going—you've shown your point of view—**unconscionable hypocrisy**—and set up an interesting contrast—**metaphors of forests and town life.**)

A thesis statement might also argue for a surprising or controversial point of view:

EXAMPLE:

The most logical and effective way to win the "drug war" in the US is to legalize all drugs and offer government-run clinics to sell and dispense all narcotics.

You've hooked your reader. Your job now? You must prove your point of view in the rest of the essay.

To arrive at your thesis statement, spend about five minutes developing a mind-map (GPS) for your document. You'll discover your point of view, and you can synthesize what you've mindstormed into a cohesive, effective statement that tells the reader what to expect in the whole essay. And your voice will shine through right from the get-go.

NOTE: Every paragraph needs a mini-thesis statement that alerts the reader to the paragraph's controlling idea.

41

Use
words
to
paint
an original,
intriguing

world.

I BELIEVE MORE IN THE SCISSORS

THAN I DO IN THE PENCIL. TRUMAN CAPOTE

through

Cut extra words ~~that you don't need~~.

USE AS FEW WORDS AS POSSIBLE.

CUT. CUT AGAIN.
NOW CUT SOME MORE.

Why?

If you want to get your point across, you must keep your reader with you.

So make your writing easy to follow.

No one wants to read long-winded sentences.
Declutter.
Get rid of unneeded words.

Let your ideas be complex.
Keep your writing simple.

The more layered and intricate your ideas, the more you need to keep your writing simple.

Let's look at some examples:

1. BEFORE: Other major architectural events also took place that same year. (10 words)

    AFTER: Other major architectural events ~~also~~ took place that ~~same~~ year. (8 words)

2. BEFORE: Our House and Grounds Committee is currently in the process of trying to obtain some more information on what is being proposed. (22 words)

    AFTER: Our House and Grounds Committee is ~~currently in the process of~~ trying to obtain ~~some~~ more information on ~~what is being proposed~~ the proposal. (14 words)

3. BEFORE: I will be picking up the printed fliers regarding the upcoming lecture sometime on Wednesday, September 17, at which time I will then be dropping off a copy for you at your office. (33 words)

    AFTER: I will ~~be~~ picking up the ~~printed~~ lecture fliers ~~regarding the upcoming lecture sometime~~ on Wednesday, September 17 ~~at which time I~~ and will ~~then be~~ dropping off a copy ~~for you~~ at your office. (20 words)

4. BEFORE: From the very beginning of our country through the depths of the 1800's, farming was the main stronghold of our country. Farming was the source of wealth and economy. (29 words)

    AFTER: From the ~~very~~ beginning of our country through ~~the depths of~~ the 1800's, farming was the main ~~stronghold of our country. Farming was the~~ source of wealth ~~and economy~~. (16 words)

5. BEFORE: In the 1920's, Americans faced many new challenges. The challenges they faced covered a wide range of issues varying from alcohol use to consequences of technology. (26 words)

    AFTER: In the 1920's, Americans faced many new challenges~~. The challenges they faced covered a wide range of issues varying~~ <u>ranging</u> from alcohol use to consequences of technology. (16 words)

REWRITE, DELETING UNNECESSARY WORDS:

1. BEFORE: In order to describe the form that Donne gives to true love, he chooses to create a scene of separation. (20 words)

AFTER:

2. BEFORE: After doing a few odd jobs, and following in his father's footsteps and becoming a preacher for several years, Baldwin moved to Paris where he lived for the next four years. (31 words)

AFTER:

3. BEFORE: Baldwin was known for writing on racy subjects such as homosexuality, civil rights, and prejudices. He was a successful writer all the way up until his death in 1987, after which his works are still read today. (37 words)

AFTER:

4. BEFORE: Stanza two describes the usual reaction lovers have to separation but explains that such reactions of tears and sighs do not prove one's love but rather the opposite by suggesting that the relationship depends on a physical connection. (38 words)

AFTER:

5. BEFORE: Fear helps us to know when to fight or take a flight. Enough, often when we experience danger, our mind will tell us if we should fight or flee from that situation. Fear acts like an instinct, which will tell us what our next move should or could be. (49 words)

AFTER:

I have made this [letter] longer,
because I have not had the time
to make it shorter.

Blaise Pascal

Don't tell me the moon is shining; show me the glint of light on broken glass.
Anton Chekhov

PUT
YOUR
VERBS
TO
WORK.

...action!

camera,

(wait for it . . .)

Put your verbs to work.

IMPROVE YOUR WRITING 100%.

LIKE FEDEX DELIVERIES: OVERNIGHT.

How?

A: Magic
B: A really smart strategy

B

With a little retooling, you can razor-sharpen your sentences, ratchet up their energy level, and showcase your ideas so vigorously that you will fall in love.

(With your own writing.)

How?

One verb needs to go.

And you need to replace it with an infinite number of other verbs. But only one verb needs to go?

Yes. Which one?

Turn the page to find out.

The verb you need to avoid?

To be and all its conjugated forms, including **am, is, are,** **was, were, has been, will be.**

Actors take your places. *SHOW TIME!*

Do you want to watch a play that has no actors? Or a movie with actors who just stand there?

Let's imagine an actor who appears on stage and tells the audience, "I am mad at my boss." Then she says, "I feel the weight of the world on my shoulders." Yet nothing in her face, body language, or tone of voice convinces you. Why?

GOOD ACTORS DON'T JUST TELL. THEY SHOW.

JUST LIKE GOOD WRITERS.

For sparkling, clear, stay-with-me writing, every sentence should have an **actor** and an **action**. And the action will define the life of your writing. Just as a good actor communicates through tone, gesture, and emotion, good writers need to use verbal cues to communicate their message.

Look at this "BEFORE" example:

This morning *there was* a pretty sunrise.

Name the actor in the sentence: "There was a pretty sunrise."

Correct: no actor.

And the verb? *was*

Active, lively, energetic? No.
Because the verb *was* describes only existence.

A sunrise existed.

Now let's look at an "AFTER" sentence:

This morning when the sun rose over the horizon, the sky turned deep orange.

True, the "AFTER" sentence has more words. But which sentence does the following:

- **Grabs your interest?**
- **Puts you into the scene?**
- **Provides an actor?**
- **Tells?**
- **Shows?**

In the "AFTER" sentence we see an actor—someone or something—*doing* something!

the   ^{actor} **sun**   ^{action} **rose**

the   ^{actor} **sky**   ^{action} **turned**

Why do we find the "AFTER" sentence more effective?

In English, we process information most easily by **seeing** someone or something—what we call **the actor** in a sentence—**doing** something.

Unless you have a specific reason (we'll get to that in the next section), **keep the actor next to the action**—just as you do in everyday conversation:

Rafael ran **a marathon.**

Linda sang **an aria.**

Henry read **the book.**

What do you notice about the verbs in those sentences?
You got it:

They act.

They perform.

They have energy and focus.

Ok, sometimes, you have to use a to-be verb, as in this sentence: "Ronald is a man." The to-be verb *is* conveys the fact of Ronald's gender. To convey that fact in any other way would stretch the point: "The male gender exists in Ronald."

So use a to-be verb when necessary. Just get away from those boring, unfocused sentences as fast as possible.

See how these boring to-be sentences spring to life as active, lively sentences that show, don't tell.

1. BEFORE: It was a hot day.

  AFTER: The sun beat on the asphalt.

2. BEFORE: I was tired.

  AFTER: I dragged myself through the door.

3. BEFORE: What is fear? Fear is something that is in everyone. All of us experience fear at some point or another. It is like an emotion that has already been with us since thousands of years ago. Why then is fear a useful emotion? (43 words; 6 to-be verbs)

  AFTER: Everyone experiences fear at some point. Knowing that humans have always felt the emotional drive of fear, we might ask if fear actually helps us. (25 words; no to-be verbs)

4. BEFORE: Whenever something we have been taught all our lives as being true is challenged, it is always met with some resistance and doubt. More so when it is historical than scientific it seems. History is usually based on human events that have taken place. Those events are written into books and passed down through people in stories. But just like a scientific breakthrough, history is all about research and discovery as well. (72 words; 8 to-be verbs)

AFTER: Whenever our lifelong beliefs <u>come</u> into question, we often <u>meet</u> these challenges with doubt. We usually <u>have</u> less resistance to changes in scientific theories than with changing historical information. The history of human events <u>passes</u> through generations and <u>becomes</u> "factual" when these accounts <u>appear</u> in history books. Yet historical accuracy, no less than scientific knowledge, <u>relies</u> on research and discovery. (60 words; no to-be verbs)

DO THIS:

- Circle every <u>to-be verb</u> in your draft.
  You will probably find a to-be verb in nearly every sentence.
- Replace every one of those <u>to-be verbs</u> with an active verb.
  You may have to restructure your sentence, but you'll have a much better sentence.
- Rewrite every sentence that begins with a <u>to-be construction</u> (It is... There were...).
  In other words: **Never start a sentence with a to-be verb.**

Now see your writing dramatically improve 100%.

EXERCISES

1. Find the verbs

FROM *SEABISCUIT* BY LAURA HILLENBRAND

Circle the verb or verbs in each sentence. Note how Hillenbrand takes you into the scene so you race right along with Seabiscuit, never lagging for a moment. Identify the actor/action relationship in each sentence.

[Pollard is the jockey riding Seabiscuit; Velociter and Uppermost are two horses in the race.]

Starting his race all alone, Pollard tried to run the incident to his advantage, cutting in to the rail for a ground-saving trip while far ahead of him, Velociter and Uppermost cruised to the lead. Pollard unleashed Seabiscuit's rally immediately, rushing up behind the field in hopes of finding an avenue through the pack. As the first turn approached, the horses farther out from the rail hustled inward and cut Seabiscuit off. With nowhere to go, Pollard waited. They pulled toward the backstretch, and Pollard saw a narrow hole open between horses and tried to send Seabiscuit through it. He didn't make it, and had to snatch up the reins and yank Seabiscuit back to prevent him from clipping the heels of the horses coming together in front of him. Trapped again, Pollard waited until the field straightened out. A hole opened. Pollard told Seabiscuit to take it, and the horse darted in.

Seabiscuit shot through the pack, swung out, and drew ahead of Uppermost, claiming second on the outside. Only front-running Velociter remained to be caught. Tugging his right rein, Pollard fanned his colt out and hung on as Seabiscuit gunned Velociter down. All alone again, but this time in front, Pollard leaned back and slowed Seabiscuit for the last fifty yards. They cantered down the lane and hit the wire, winners by five lengths.

2. Re-Write

Rewrite the following paragraph to replace to-be verbs with strong, active verbs. Get rid of unnecessary words as you work on the to-be verbs.

Kids for Life is a volunteer organization that provides services to unaccompanied minors who are living on the streets. There is one serious misconception about kids who are out there living on the streets, and that is that they want to be there. It is not something they choose when they are in a good living environment when they are living in the home. These kids quickly find out that the street is not a friendly place to live, and if they are choosing that life, it is because they left behind something that is a lot worse. The dangers of drugs, robbery, and sexual assault are there regardless of whether or not someone is designated officially homeless. (15 to-be verbs; 118 words total)

(Adapted from "Volunteering with Street Youth," *Spare Change News,* Boston, MA, July 2010)

3. Free-Write (150-250 words)

Tell a story about one of these photos, using the writing principles you've learned so far. Use your imagination! Use only action verbs (try to avoid to-be verbs altogether). Keep the actor next to the action.

Write powerful sentences

ng, will ya?

Avoid passive sentences.

5

PASSIVE CONSTRUCTIONS

EVERY SENTENCE COMPRISES THREE ELEMENTS:

1. Subject
2. Verb
3. Complete idea

FOR EXAMPLE:

subject	verb	direct object
Seth	**rides**	**the bike.**

The subject—**Seth**—performs an action—**rides**—(the verb). The direct object—**the bike**—completes the idea.

The writer has created an active construction by placing the actor and the action next to each other in the sentence.

We see Seth doing something.

But when should you *not* provide that strong, clear actor/action arrangement?

Only two times:

1. You can *effectively* use a passive construction when you don't want to call attention to the actor because the action reflects poorly on the actor.

FOR EXAMPLE:

actor   action
The committee **will raise** fees for the event.

The actor = the committee
The action = will raise
The direct object: fees

But the committe doesn't want to take the hit for raising the fees. How about this convenient change:

Fees for the event will be raised.

Who raised the fees? (The committee stays out of the sentence.)

No actor = a passive construction.

In a passive construction, the subject doesn't perform the action. <u>The subject doesn't act</u>.

The subject just sits there passively. The action takes place without an actor.

Awkward and unnatural, right?

subject   verb
Fees   **will be raised.**

The subject—the fees—await an action: to be raised. (But no one raises them—no actor.)

And you see the verb? <u>will be</u>.

No one—no actor—in the sentence performs an action.

NOTE: Sometimes an actor does appear in a passive construction, but only at the end of the sentence:

subject   verb
The bed   **was made**   *by Jenny*.

2. You can *effectively* use a passive construction when the direct object takes precedence over the actor in importance.

FOR EXAMPLE:

Barack Obama was elected.

Who elected him? The people. The people elected Barack Obama. (An active construction, but the spotlight really ought to fall on the direct object: Barack Obama.)

The important information? Who won the election. The reader already knows that the people elected him.

How to identify a passive sentence:

1. look for to-be verbs
2. look for sentences that end with the construction "by _____. (The book <u>was</u> written <u>by Ernest Hemingway</u>.)

do something, will ya: do

So—use passive constructions in only two situations:

1. When you don't want to identify the actor.

(Bad news and the actor doesn't want the spotlight.)

2. When the direct object takes precedence in importance over the actor.

Passive constructions almost always use **to-be verbs**, so get away from these boring, unfocused sentences as fast as possible. Ask yourself, Who or what is the actor of the sentence? Is the sentence missing an actor? (Passive for sure!) If the sentence does have an actor, does it come before or after the action? For clear, active sentences, the **actor** should come **before** the **action**!

EXAMPLES from actual college essays at the website www.antiessays.com

1. BEFORE: It is possible for children to be pulled into the television's realistic world of violence with sometimes devastating results.
(19 words; two to-be verbs—passive)

Who pulls children into the world of television violence? Who or what is the actor?

　　　　　　　actor　　　　　action　　　　　　　　　action
　AFTER: Television violence can attract children and cause devastating effects. (9 words; no to-be verbs—active)

2. BEFORE: Many outside factors were believed to affect the Civil War's outcome. (11 words; one to-be verb—passive)

Who believed that outside factors affected the outcome of the Civil War? Who or what is the actor?

　　　　　　actor　　　　action
　AFTER: Historians believed that many outside factors affected the outcome of the Civil War. (13 words; no to-be verbs—active)

3. BEFORE: The Chesapeake Bay was explored in 1609 by Captain John Smith. By the mid-seventeenth century the area now known as Maryland was organized as a colony. (26 words; two to-be verbs—passive)

In the first sentence, the actor comes at the end of the sentence "by Captain John Smith." In the second sentence, who organized the area now known as Maryland as a colony? Who or what is the actor?

　　　　　　　　　　actor　　　　　　　action
　AFTER: In 1609, Captain John Smith explored the Chesapeake Bay. By the mid-17th century,

actor　　　action
settlers organized the area now known as Maryland as a colony.
(24 words; no to-be verbs—active)

ALL STYLES ARE GOOD, EXCEPT THE BORING.

Voltaire

Don't make your readers
guess who you're talking
about.

MAKE SURE YOUR READER DOESN'T GET CONFUSED WHEN YOU USE A PRONOUN.

who?

Put pronouns in their place.

You talkin' to me?

Don't make your readers guess who does what.

Pronouns take the place of a noun.

BUT UNDERSTAND:
A pronoun refers to the appropriate noun that immediately precedes it. This noun is called the pronoun's antecedent (ante = before).

Follow this principle, and you will never confuse your reader.

EXAMPLES:

Shauna baked a cake. She likes to cook.

Who likes to cook? Has to be Shauna. Shauna is the closest and only appropriate antecedent to the pronoun *she*.

Shauna and Susan baked a cake. She likes to cook.

Who likes to cook? In this sentence the *closest* proper noun—the antecedent—is Susan. If you mean Shauna likes to cook, not Susan, you have to reintroduce Shauna:

Shauna and Susan baked a cake. Shauna likes to cook.

Make sure your reader doesn't get confused when you use a pronoun.

Again: When you use a pronoun, its antecedent will be the closest noun that agrees with the gender or number of your pronoun.

EXAMPLES:

1. Shauna and Charles baked a cake. She likes to cook.
(No confusion because of the specific gender of the pronoun—only one female noun in the sentence.)

2. Shauna and Charles baked a cake. He likes to cook.
(No confusion because of the specific gender of the pronoun—only one male noun in the sentence.)

3. Shauna and Charles baked a cake. They like to cook.
(No confusion. Two subject nouns, one plural pronoun.)

4. Shauna and Charles baked a cake for their parents. They like to cook.
Who likes to cook? The antecedent to *they* is *parents* (closest noun that agrees with the pronoun). Do you mean that the parents or Shauna and Charles like to cook? If you mean Shauna and Charles, then you have to reintroduce them.

Shauna and Charles baked a cake for their parents. Shauna and Charles like to cook.

Who: Put pronouns in their place.

5. The Nelsons invited their neighbors over for a barbecue. They have not been too friendly in the past.
(The Nelsons or the neighbors have not been friendly? Has to be neighbors, the closest appropriate antecedent to the pronoun *they*.)

But if that's not what you mean, you have to clarify for the reader:

The Nelsons invited their neighbors over for a barbecue. The Nelsons have not been too friendly in the past.

6. The Bronte sisters wrote novels filled with passion. They have since become icons of the English-speaking world.
(The Bronte sisters or the novels? The pronoun *they* must refer to its closest appropriate antecedent, *novels*. If you mean the Bronte sisters, you must reintroduce them.)

The Bronte sisters wrote novels filled with passion. The sisters have since become icons of the English-speaking world.

Even if you mean the novels, just to avoid confusion, reintroduce the noun you refer to:

The Bronte sisters wrote novels filled with passion. These novels have since become icons of the English-speaking world.

Make sure **pronouns agree** in **gender** and **number** with their antecedents.

7. You may not want to become part of organized religion, but many people get a lot of help from them.

Them, a plural pronoun, grammatically agrees with its closest antecedent, *people*. But the writer means *organized religion*, which is a singular noun.

You may not want to become part of organized religion, but many people get a lot of help from religious groups.

Often writers think it's okay to "get away" with faulty pronoun references because the reader "will get the idea."

DON'T MAKE YOUR READER WORK TO UNDERSTAND YOUR MEANING.

Precision in writing means your reader will zip right through your prose without faltering, stopping, or having to reread.

AND YOU LOOK LIKE A GENIUS.

Trace every pronoun—including *it*, *that*, *which*, *this*, *these*, *those*—back to its closest antecedent: 'the noun it replaces Sometimes these words serve different functions in a sentence besides being pronouns. To find out if you're using them as pronouns, ask yourself if they function as the subject (or actor) of the sentence. If they do, then you must check to ensure that they relate correctly to their antecedent.

If any confusion could arise, rewrite the sentence.

Put pronouns in their place.

WHO?

Look at these two examples from an online college term paper website—www.termpaperslab.com. The website boasts that it offers students "high-quality term papers." Hmmm....

1. BEFORE: The exaggeration of fear or fear mongering is used widespread in movies everyday to promote and instill fear in <u>its</u> audiences.

Who or what does *its* refer to?

   AFTER: Filmmakers use fear tactics in their movies to instill fear in the audience. (Once you break down this sentence does it really mean anything?)

2. BEFORE: Everybody knows that Henry Aaron held the record for the most career home runs. But most of <u>them</u> probably do not know that he still holds the record for the most career Runs Batted In (RBIs) with 2297.

What does *them* refer to? *Home runs*? Do you think the writer means *home runs*?

   AFTER: Most people know that Henry Aaron held the record for most career home runs. But probably <u>most people</u> don't know that he still holds the record for the most runs batted in (2297).

Look at this example from *The Story of English* by McCrum, MacNeil, and Cran (p. 277):

3. BEFORE: After the Civil War was over and the Union had been made safe, <u>it</u> became the American dream to unite the country in fact as well as in rhetoric.

Who or what does *it* refer to?

   AFTER: After the Civil War ended and the Union had been made safe, <u>Americans dreamed</u> of uniting the country in fact as well as in rhetoric.

Make sure you clarify exactly what you refer to if there could be more than one antecedent.

BEFORE: Thomas Jefferson wrote about the separation of church and state, designed his own home at Monticello, became an ambassador to France, and wrote the Declaration of Independence. That is why he is one of the most important figures in U.S. history.

AFTER: Thomas Jefferson wrote about the separation of church and state, designed his own home at Monticello, became an ambassador to France, and wrote the Declaration of Independence. These accomplishments make him one of the most important figures in U.S. history.

OR

AFTER: Thomas Jefferson wrote about the separation of church and state, designed his own home at Monticello, became an Ambassador to France, and wrote the Declaration of Independence. His writing of the Declaration of Independence makes him one of the most important figures in U.S. history.

Other examples of this and that used as pronouns

As she left the room, Helene slammed the door. That was the last straw for Jason. (The antecedent of "that" = "Helene slammed the door.")

The company required all employees to work on New Year's Eve. Everyone thought that was so unfair. (The antecedent of "that" = "all employees had to work on New Year's Eve.")

When Buddy's mom caught him with chocolate on his face, he lied and said it was only dirt. This was his big mistake. (The antecedent of "this" = "he lied and said it was only dirt.")

Put pronouns in their place.

whom

DON'T let your reader float away

DO
keep your sentences grounded

avoid abstract
say wha

language

Use concrete language.

Use concrete language.

WRITE IT THE WAY YOU WOULD SAY IT

(IN A PROFESSIONAL CONVERSATION)

Keep your writing reader-friendly!
Follow the **Golden Rule:**
Put yourself in your reader's shoes.

You don't want to read a sentence twice.

And neither does your reader.

You don't want to reread to figure out how the last sentence relates to the opening sentence.

Your reader doesn't want to backtrack, either.

Cardinal rule:
Keep your reader in mind.

Your reader will happily stay with you if you follow these principles:

- Use concrete, specific language.
- Avoid highfalutin words. Prefer plain words.
- Provide necessary information.

Which example conveys the information most effectively (avoids follow-up questions from the reader)?

A: A meeting will be held next week to discuss several options before the committee. Please confirm if you will attend.

B: The Picnic Day Committee will meet Tuesday, May 2, at 7:00 p.m. in the fourth floor Student Lounge. We will discuss the new parking restriction, as well as the situation with the trash left on the grass after last year's Picnic Day. Please email Joanne at jojo@collegelife.edu by Monday to confirm if you will attend. Or call her at 555-555-5555.

Your reader won't have questions, because you anticipated them and answered them.

EXAMPLES from actual college essays:

1. BEFORE: Kasimir Malevich developed a radical and avant-garde aesthetic system, Suprematism, which sought to liberate painting from its historically mimetic function. (20 highfalutin, abstract words)

  AFTER: Kasimir Malevich developed a radical new system of painting, which he called Suprematism. He invented this system to free art from the tradition of realism. (25 plain, concrete words)

2. BEFORE: [From the website www.exampleessays.com]
Hitchcock's work always presented an unmistakable worldview that controlled his audience to the point that they were truly at his mercy. Hitchcock's worldview was bound up with cinematic language and created a relationship with the spectator of the film. (39 words; highfalutin, abstract language and no specific detail.)

AFTER: Hitchcock's films often center on his view that we can never know who to trust. An atmosphere of increasing doom keeps the audience constantly in suspense as Hitchcock uses techniques such as half-shadow and off-kilter camera angles. (37 words; plain language and specific detail)

3. BEFORE: I will be visiting the campus next month and need to make an appointment with your office. Can you tell me your hours and if someone will be there during the week. (32 words; not enough specific detail)

AFTER: I will be on campus during the week of May 20-25. I would like to make an appointment with a financial aid counselor to discuss arrangements for fall semester 2010. I will be a freshman. Please let me know what documents I need to bring and the best time for me to call for an appointment. I would like to meet with someone after 1:00 p.m. (67 words. No follow up needed—you have outlined specifically your needs and anticipated the reader's questions. You won't waste time when you get there because you might not have the right documents with you.)

4. BEFORE: Since the dawn of time, humans have tried to express themselves. Archeologists have found evidence that early people made different kinds of decorative artifacts. These people must have wanted to be creative. (32 words; no specific detail.)

AFTER: As early as 50,000 years ago, humans created art. For example, archeologists have discovered cave paintings and rock art in Africa, Australia, North America, Asia, South Asia, Europe, and South America. Probably the most famous, the Paleolithic cave paintings in Lascaux, in southern France, date back about 16,000 years. (49 words; you have provided specific, concrete detail.)

AN OUNCE OF EXAMPLE

BEATS ~~IS WORTH~~ A POUND
OF GENERALITIES.

HENRY JAMES

Most people won't realize

that writing is a craft.

You have to take your apprenticeship in it like anything else.

Katherine Ann Porter

upt yourself

Keep related ideas together.

DO NOT INTERRUPT YOUR MAIN POINT.

DO KEEP RELATED IDEAS NEXT TO EACH OTHER.

DO PUT EXTRA ELEMENTS ELSEWHERE IN THE SENTENCE.

Every sentence should have at least one core element: a subject, a verb, and a complete idea.

Jesse drove the truck.

Subject: <u>Jesse</u>

Verb: <u>drove</u>   = *a complete idea*

Direct object: <u>the truck</u>

REMIND YOURSELF: "KEEP RELATED IDEAS TOGETHER."

What's your point?

The hub, the nub, the nerve center, the central point, the main idea, ground zero, the sweet spot of your sentence: By whatever name, don't break it up.

Keep your main idea intact. Put extra information before or after the core element of your sentence:

EXAMPLES:

1. Big Slim won the race.
(the main idea)

2. <u>Big Slim</u>, a long shot, for the first time <u>won the race</u>.
(interrupted main idea)

3. A long shot, <u>Big Slim won the race</u> for the first time.
(main idea intact; extra information before and after)

4. <u>Big Slim won the race</u> for the first time. He ran as a longshot.
(main idea intact; extra information comes after)

In each example below:
- Name the actor, action, and direct object
- Identify the main idea.

1. BEFORE: <u>Jesse</u>, my roommate, dressed in his groomsman's tux, <u>rode</u> across the lawn in front of the Admin building on <u>his bike</u>.

  AFTER: Dressed in his groomsman's tux, <u>Jesse rode his bike</u> across the lawn in front of the Admin building.

2. BEFORE: <u>Jesse rode</u> without both hands on the handlebars on <u>his bike</u>.

   AFTER: <u>Jesse rode his bike</u> without both hands on the handlebars.

3. BEFORE: I hate tuna, but if she would **make the sandwich**, <u>I told his sister</u>, **on rye bread**, <u>I would eat</u> it.

   AFTER: I hate tuna, but <u>I told his sister I would eat the sandwich</u> if she would **make it on rye bread**.

4. BEFORE: <u>Faulkner and Hemingway</u> both <u>wrote</u> during the 1920s and 1930s <u>with passion about their subjects</u>, which were landmark decades in American history.

   AFTER: <u>Faulkner and Hemingway both wrote passionately about their subjects</u> during the 1920s and 1930s, which were landmark decades in American history.
   (put related ideas next to each other)
   or
   AFTER: During the 1920s and 1930s, which were landmark decades in American history, <u>Faulkner and Hemingway both wrote passionately about their subjects</u>.

5. BEFORE: When the story begins, <u>Holden</u>, at age sixteen, due to his poor grades, <u>is kicked out</u> of Pencey Prep, a boys' school in Pennsylvania.

   AFTER: When the story begins, 16-year-old <u>Holden gets kicked out</u> of Pencey Prep, a boys' school in Pennsylvania.

6. BEFORE: <u>I came home one evening</u> from an intensive, introductory training session at a local gym <u>in great pain</u>.

   AFTER: <u>I came home one evening in great pain</u> from an intensive, introductory training session at a local gym.

7. BEFORE: Years ago, when <u>most people</u> could not read or write <u>in Africa</u> ...

   AFTER: Years ago, when <u>most people in Africa</u> could not read or write ...

EXERCISES

1. Find the actor, action, and direct object

Identify the actor, action, and direct object of each sentence. Underline the main assertion. Does every sentence keep the main assertion intact, with supplementary information goes either before or after the main idea? If not, identify the problem.

Excerpted from the article "People Making a Difference: Lyndon Harris" (about Father Lyndon Harris, former parish priest at St. Paul's Chapel, Ground Zero) by Marilyn Jones, *The Christian Science Monitor*, July 27, 2009

All the children and their parents working nearby survived [the attacks on the World Trade Center]. For Harris, the day went by in a blur. He spent most of it on the street, helping. The next morning, still dazed, he arrived at little St. Paul's Chapel, just up the street from Trinity. Ashes covered the cemetery out back, but the 200-year-old sanctuary where George Washington once worshiped was intact.

As the newly appointed priest in charge of St. Paul's, Harris made a decision. With his superiors at Trinity out of town, he spontaneously opened the chapel to the hundreds of workers at ground zero. For eight months, St. Paul's became a refuge to firefighters, workers, heavy-equipment operators, and police officers.

Open 24 hours a day, St. Paul's served more than a half million meals. Counselors, musicians, and an untold number of volunteers from around the world helped. The grimy faces and worn bodies of the workers showed the strain of their bleak work. But the smiles and uplifted waves to news cameras also revealed how profoundly touched these workers felt by the outpouring of love. Cards, letters, posters, quilts, and pictures hung from every fence, surface, pew, and wall of the "little chapel that stood."

2. Free-Write (150-250 words)

Tell a story about this photo, using the writing principles you've learned so far. **Use your imagination!**

When something can be read without effort,
great effort has gone into its writing.

— Enrique Jardiel Poncela

Sentences create the melodic

Words are the notes.

/ Eliot Plum

]

line of a writer's music.

flow

state

Move smoothly from sentence to sentence.

You know when you read a piece of writing and you just don't stop reading? Because each sentence flows so beautifully to the next, each idea streams seamlessly to the next?

Writers don't write prose like that in a first draft. That kind of writing takes polishing. And the careful writer, the one who makes writing look easy—and a pleasure to read—knows a few tricks to get you, the reader, to stay right there on the page.

You don't become distracted because this writer has got you.

Want to know how?

FLOW STATE WRITING:

Sentences that flow naturally from idea to idea without breaking the reader's rhythm and concentration depend on how the writer presents information.

Two principles:

1. Transition information goes at the beginning of a sentence
2. New information goes at the end of a sentence

Herky-jerky writing: **Abraham Lincoln freed the slaves and is revered by people around the world. He wasn't always an avid abolitionist, but still most African Americans consider him a hero.**

What are the important pieces of information in those two sentences?

1. **Abraham Lincoln freed the slaves**
2. **He wasn't always an avid abolitionist**

REWRITE:

new information
People around the world revere Abraham Lincoln because <u>he freed the slaves</u>.

transitional information (refers back to <u>slaves</u> in previous sentence)
Today, <u>most of their descendants</u> consider him a hero, even though

new information
<u>he wasn't always an avid abolitionist</u>.

Note how "<u>most of their descendants</u>"refers back to (has a transitional relationship with) "the slaves."

The *new* information comes at the end of the sentence: "even though <u>he wasn't always an avid abolitionist</u>."

117

Keep this flow state going:

transitional information (refers back to Lincoln being an abolitionist)
While <u>the issue of abolition</u> divided the United States during Lincoln's presidency,

new information   transitional information
in the end, Lincoln's stand <u>cost him his life</u>. <u>Assassinated just days after</u> the close of the war,

new information
<u>Lincoln became the symbol of a country ripped apart by war.</u>

transitional information (refers back to war)
<u>Many of the wounds of that conflict</u> remain today, even though

new information
<u>civil rights</u> for all Americans have improved significantly since the 1860s.

Bottom line:

Put transitional information at the beginning of the sentence.

Save the new—and most important—information for the back of the sentence.

When you write like this, your reader will stay with you start to finish.

Your writing will flow like silk.

You just gotta know the tricks.

The idea is to write it

and   it   slides

and   goes   straight

so that people hear it

through the brain

to the heart.

strong

Make a good last impression.

10

finish strong

Make a good last impression.

DON'T END ON A FLAT TIRE.

DO END WITH A JACK-KNIFE DIVE, STRAIGHT INTO THE WATER.

And make it a

ten.

finish strong

Make a good last impression.

You've brought your reader through your well-thought-out essay.

You've followed all the principles of the All-Nighter Writer:

- You've opened strong
- Your sentences flow, one idea smoothly transitioning to the next
- Your actors act, your actions zing
- You've even provided road signs along the way— correct punctuation (See Chapter 10)

Now what?

A predictable, boring, wrap-it-up ending that leaves your reader backstroking for shore?

Not a chance!

You need to conclude your essay as strongly as you opened it.

GIVE YOUR READER A FEEL-GOOD KICK IN THE PANTS.

Your conclusion should surprise your reader. But it should also have the ring of inevitability. **Not an easy trick.**

But let's look at some ways you can weed out the amateur conclusions.

Clichés and typical mistakes to avoid:
- "In conclusion…."
- "To sum up…."
- "In summary…"
- Restate the opening (in different words, but basically the same ideas)
- Open up a whole new topic
- End abruptly, with no concluding idea
- Drag on with what you've already said throughout the essay

If writing a dynamic conclusion were easy, everyone would do it, right?

EXAMPLE OF A GREAT ENDING:

From Frank Rich's column in *The New York Times*, July 26, 2009: "And That's Not The Way It Is."

Last paragraph from Rich's column about how the media has failed to follow the example of Walter Cronkite's reporting style and how Cronkite kept his distance from Washington insiders (the salons):

"Watching many of the empty Cronkite tributes in his own medium over the past week, you had to wonder if his industry was sticking to mawkish clichés just to avoid unflattering comparisons. If he was the most trusted man in America, it wasn't because he was a nice guy with an authoritative voice and a lived-in face. It wasn't because he "loved a good story" or that he removed his glasses when a president died. It was because at a time of epic corruption in the most powerful precincts in Washington, Cronkite was not at the salons and not in the tank."

Note that the column ends on the hard consonant "k"—and the short, abrupt word "tank" reverberates because it takes the reader by surprise. And "in the tank" sums up the point of the whole column: The current media—unlike Conkrite —are "in the tank"(with the politicians). A surprise twist, but also an inevitable conclusion.

So don't stumble at the finish line.

I can't say it better than Roy Peter Clark, who pictures a writer as a dismounting gymnast:

"Stick the landing with a twist."

In other words— SAVE THE BEST FOR LAST.

Writing succeeds when it puts pictures
inside our heads,
when it makes it possible for us to
visualize people and landscapes,
actions and scenes.
We remember what we can visualize.
We think about what we can
remember.

Lauren Kessler

CLEAR? CONCRETE? DOWN TO EARTH?

DID YOU SAVE THE BEST FOR LAST?

ns

Learn these four must-know rules of punctuation.

11

road signs

Learn these four must-know rules of punctuation.

RULE #1:
SEVEN COORDINATING CONJUNCTIONS

FANBOYS: FOR AND NOR BUT OR YET SO

A sentence with two independent clauses joined by a coordinating conjunction always requires a comma before the conjunction.

I bought the ticket, and I saw the movie.

"I bought the ticket" stands alone because the clause has a subject (I), a verb (bought), and expresses a complete idea ("I bought a ticket").

"I saw the movie" also stands alone as an independent clause: It has a subject (I), a verb (saw), and the clause expresses a complete idea (I saw a movie).

These two independent clauses have been joined to create a compound sentence *coordinated* by the conjunction "and." Since "and" joins two independent clauses, the sentence requires a comma before the conjunction.

The comma signals a pause because the reader has just processed a full sentence—the first half of the compound sentence, which has a subject, verb, and complete idea. The comma indicates a pause because now here comes another full sentence with its own subject, verb, and complete idea.

A sentence with a conjunction doesn't always require a comma. The conjunction must coordinate two complete clauses.

road signs

For example:

I bought the ticket and saw the movie.

This sentence *does not take a comma* before the conjunction. Why? Here, the conjunction "and" *does not coordinate* two complete clauses. The phrase "and saw the movie" does not stand alone. It depends on the first clause for its subject, *I*. This sentence does not require a pause because the reader needs one element—the subject—in the first part of the sentence to understand the second half of the sentence.

Marina wrote the ad, and Stephanie presented it.
(two independent clauses coordinated by the conjunction *and*)

Marina wrote the ad and presented it.
(An independent clause and a dependent phrase. No subject in the second half of the sentence. Therefore, no comma is required.)

Easy tips:
- When proofing, look for FANBOYS in all sentences.
- If a full sentence follows one of the FANBOYS—the sentence will always take a comma before the conjunction.
- If the clause or phrase following one of the FANBOYS is missing either a subject, a verb, or is not a complete idea, the sentence does **not** take a comma before the conjunction.

FOR AND NOR BUT OR YET SO

RULE #2:
SEMICOLONS

Use a semicolon to separate two independent clauses with no conjunction to coordinate them, and only if the clauses are closely related in idea. If the second clause is not closely related in idea to the first clause, break the clauses into two sentences and use a period to separate them.

Use semicolons sparingly. They annoy the reader. (And don't use them with coordinating conjunctions.)

Jeremy sang the lead; Belinda provided backup.
(closely related ideas)

Jeremy sang the lead. Belinda arrived late for the cast party.
(not closely related ideas)

We made it all the way to Baltimore without stopping for food; Jon brought along chips and salsa.

We made it all the way to Baltimore without stopping for food. Jon found out that the Ravens lost.

Easy tip: If the sentence has a conjunction—a FANBOY—the sentence will not take a semicolon.

The only other time to use a semicolon:
When you have groups of items separated by commas, separate the groups by semicolons.

We brought the camping supplies to the staging center: tents, bags, towels, pillows; stoves, canteens, utensils; repellent, first-aid kits, and bandages.

Another tip: If you want to group items into sets, be sure to group them by category.

RULE #3:
INTRODUCTORY DEPENDENT CLAUSE

When a dependent phrase or clause *introduces* an independent clause, place a comma *before* the independent clause. (You don't need a comma for a dependent phrase that *follows* the independent clause.)

introductory dependent clause (requires comma)
If you want to learn to write, you should take the All-Nighter Writer course.

independent clause with dependent clause following (no comma)
You should take the All-Nighter Writer course if you want to learn to write.

introductory dependent clause (requires comma)
When I feel sleepy in my classes, I try not to sit up front.

independent clause with dependent clause following (no comma)
I try not to sit up front when I get sleepy in my classes.

introductory dependent clause (requires comma)

<u>On test days</u>, I usually run a mile.

independent clause with dependent phrase following (no comma)

I usually run a mile <u>on test days</u>.

Easy tip: Look for prepositions that start sentences. (Prepositions show location, time, and relationships between objects. For example, *when*, *after*, *before*, *in*, *on*, *upon*, *by*, *with*, *under*.) Starting a sentence with a preposition means you have a dependent introductory clause or phrase, which will require a comma before the following independent clause.

RULE #4:
PARENTHETICAL ELEMENTS

When you have a word or group of words that you can delete entirely from the sentence without changing the meaning or the grammatical construction of the sentence, enclose those words with either commas, parentheses, or dashes.

Choose commas to indicate the least interruption in the flow of the sentence.

Abraham Lincoln, the 16th president, grew up in Illinois.

Choose parentheses to indicate that the information is more or less an aside, as if you're just adding information that's not all that important but you decided to include it anyway.

Chan's whole family (including his two aunts) will attend the graduation.

Choose dashes to indicate that you want to call attention to this added information—that you consider this a "wow" factor in the sentence.

No one knew that Steven—the youngest winner in the tournament's history—had never competed before that day.

Remember that the information you enclose can be removed entirely from the sentence without changing the meaning of the sentence.

My brother, William, did not go to college.

How many brothers do you have? If you have just one brother and his name is William then you enclose his name with commas.

Why?

Because you can remove his name and you will not change the meaning or the grammatical construction of the sentence.

This is called <u>non-restrictive information</u>. You don't need the name William to correctly identify your subject (my only brother).

My brother did not go to college.

The reader doesn't have to know your brother's name to know that your only brother did not go to college.

However, if you have more than one brother, one named William, one named Terrance, and the other named Hugo, then you cannot enclose the name William with commas.

Why?

Because the reader must know which brother you mean. Your brother William did not go to college.

But your other brother Hugo did go to college.

So you cannot remove the name William, because if you do, you will change the meaning of the sentence. William is necessary for your reader to know which brother you're referring to.

This is called <u>restrictive information</u>. William provides the necessary information to correctly identify your subject (my brother).

- My brother William did not go to college.
- My brother Hugo did go to college.
- My brother Terrance is in ninth grade.

EXAMPLES: Punctuation required (see answers below)

1. My favorite writer William Shakespeare lived in the 1600s.
2. The class which started with 25 students now has only 12 people attending.
3. My sister Emilia lives in Sacramento; my twin sister Shannon lives in Nashville.
4. The books on the shelf near the door belong to the library.
5. Are you aware that Troy Harrison recently hired as an intern by Focus Films has changed his major to drama?
6. In his novel *The Sound and The Fury* William Faulkner explores family life in the South.
7. When Spielberg directed his first Oscar-winning film *Shindler's List* he shot only one scene with color.
8. I grew up in the blue house on the corner of Monroe Street and Washington Avenue in downtown Auburn.
9. He began his singing career if you can call it that at an Elvis impersonation fair.
10. Please bring your laptops or bluebooks I prefer laptops to the exam on Thursday.

ANSWERS

1. My favorite writer, William Shakespeare, lived in the 1600s.
I have only one favorite writer. His name is William Shakespeare. But you don't have to know his name to know that my favorite writer lived in the 1600s. You can remove his name entirely without changing the meaning or grammatical construction of the sentence. (My favorite writer lived in the 1600s.)

2. The class, which started with 25 students, now has only 12 people attending.
The main idea: The class now has only 12 people attending. The fact that the class started with 25 students is not restrictive information. You can delete it altogether without changing the meaning of the sentence or its grammatical construction.

road signs

Tip: "Which" always means nonrestrictive information and therefore always takes a comma; "that" means the information following is restrictive and never takes a comma. (More on "which hunting" in All-Nighter Writer, Volume 2.)

3. My sister Emilia lives in Sacramento; my twin sister, Shannon, lives in Nashville.

In the first clause, since I have more than one sister, I would not use commas to set off Emilia. You need to know that I have more than one sister—and one of my sisters lives in Sacramento.

In the second clause, I've said I have a twin sister. Her name is Shannon. You know I must have only one twin sister. So my twin sister—and by the way her name is Shannon—lives in Nashville. But you don't need to know Shannon's name to know that my only twin sister lives in Nashville. In the first clause, you cannot remove Emilia's name to clearly identify your subject. But you can remove Shannon's name because it's not necessary to clearly identify "my only twin sister." So, no commas to set off Emilia's name, but commas or parentheses to set off Shannon's name.

4. The books on the shelf near the door belong to the library.

No commas to set of "on the shelf near the door." You might think I mean the books on the bookcase or the books on the floor or the books on the table. Therefore, I cannot set off "on the shelf near the door" with commas because I need that restrictive information to clearly identify the subject: the books on the shelf near the door.

5. Are you aware that Troy Harrison, recently hired as an intern by Focus Films, has changed his major to drama?

We set off the information that Troy was recently hired as an intern by Focus Films because it is not restrictive information. You don't need to have that information to clearly understand that Troy changed his major to drama.

6. In his novel *The Sound and The Fury*, William Faulkner explores family life in the South.

No commas surround the title *The Sound and The Fury* because Faulkner wrote more than one novel. If we put a comma after novel, it would indicate that the title can be removed because Faulkner wrote just one novel, and we don't need the name of the novel. But Faulkner wrote many novels; therefore, the title must be retained here to clearly identify which novel we're talking about.

BTW: The comma following the title punctuates the introductory dependent phrase (see Rule # 3).

145

7. When Spielberg directed his first Oscar-winning film, *Schindler's List*, he shot only one scene with color.

Here we do enclose the title *Schindler's List* because Spielberg had only one film that was his first Oscar-winning film. He directed many films, but only one that garnered his first Oscar.

8. I grew up in the blue house on the corner of Monroe Street and Washington Avenue in downtown Auburn.

"On the corner of Monroe Street and Washington Avenue" cannot be removed because it is restrictive information. "I grew up in the blue house in downtown Auburn" doesn't give the reader the clear identification of which blue house you mean. No commas.

9. He began his singing career—if you can call it that—at an Elvis impersonation fair.

We enclosed this unnecessary parenthetical information with dashes to call attention to it. The writer wants the reader to know that the parenthetical information is meant to be funny.

10. Please bring your laptops or bluebooks (I prefer laptops) to the exam on Thursday.

The writer wants the reader to know that he or she prefers laptops. The aside, "I prefer laptops," is not restrictive information. That information can be set off with commas or parentheses. Neither the meaning nor the grammatical construction changes with that information deleted: Please bring your laptops or bluebooks to the exam on Thursday.

road signs

Now your turn!

Correctly punctuate these real examples from published articles.

1. When downsizing is necessary Ms. Lyman finds that the best firms "go what they consider the extra mile in providing benefits extending health insurance and making COBRA payments" which extends healthcare coverage for the unemployed.

2. Paired with a glamorous Russian dancer the prince won 75 percent of the phone in votes in the grand finale of the show.

3. Syria hopes to cut a deal with the US and signals from the White House have elicited great optimism in the country.

4. Despite a government ban on journalists working in the conflict zone some international broadcast outlets have been trying to cover the deteriorating situation in Sri Lanka

5. Tom Cruise portrays Joel Goodsen an alienated young man who like many real life Gen Xers is a latchkey kid abandoned by his vacationing parents at their suburban home.

6. Princeton Universitys Gerta Keller a paleontologist who was lead author on the study doesn't dispute that the asteroid hit and that it hurt.

nuts

&bolts

Other stuff you need to know.

12

SENTENCES

Remember this fundamental formula:

A sentence must have three elements:
1. Subject
2. Verb
3. A complete idea

Shorty threw the ball.

Subject: Shorty
Verb: threw
Complete idea: Shorty threw the ball.

A fragment lacks one of these three elements:

Shorty and the ball. (No verb)
Shorty threw over the fence. (Threw what? Not a complete idea)

A run-on sentence occurs when two complete sentences are "fused" into one sentence. (Length is not the issue; run-ons occur in both short and long sentences.)

Shorty threw the ball over the fence it was awesome.
Shorty threw the ball over the fence his dad was proud of him.
Shorty threw the ball over the fence and broke a window he ran away and hoped no one would know he was the one who broke the window.

EXAMPLES:

Re-write the following sentences to create full sentences with a subject, verb, and complete idea.

1. At the top of his game, expecting an early victory.

2. Working on the project even after the deadline.

3. Candace got the role in the play, and was her first acting gig.

4. So many times the clean-up crew found a lot of miscellaneous on the grounds.

5. Beneath the moon shining on a starry night.

CAPITALIZATION

Use capital letters in these two instances:
1. the first word of a sentence
2. a proper noun or adjective

A *proper noun* is the name of a **particular** person, place, or thing. A *proper adjective i*s a modifier derived from a proper noun, such as *American flag*.

Capitalize titles and departments to designate a **specific** individual or department. Capitalize the person's title **only if comes before the person's name**, not after.

- Vice President Singh will address the Rotary Club.

- Ram Singh, vice president of our fraternity, will organize the event.

- All vice presidents will submit their budgets by Friday.

- Send your application to Ms. Green in the Harvard Personnel Department.

- Send your application to the personnel department of several schools if you want to increase your chances.

Capitalize north, south, east, and west only when used as the **proper name of a region**:

- He thought the cuisine of the East was strange but delicious.

Do not capitalize the following:

- generic buildings: hospital, school, library

- the seasons: spring, summer, winter, fall

- adjectives derived from directions and regions: southern cooking; eastern schools.

- any part of a hyphenated compound that would not ordinarily be capitalized: English-speaking, mid-Atlantic.

- the words north, south, east, and west when designating direction. Juan lives south of the campus.

EXAMPLES:
CIRCLE THE CORRECT WORD

1. The (South, south) is a region known for its hospitality.

2. Drop your final exam at (Professor Wiggland's/professor Wiggland's) office in (North/north) Hall.

3. All classes for the (Summer, summer) session will be held in the (Student Center, student center) next to the (Faculty, faculty) parking lot.

4. Anyone with a (European/european) passport can attend free of charge. All those with (North/north) American passports will have to pay $5.

5. Dr. S.O. Borring served as our (Department's/department's) first paid speaker, even though he was (President/president) of the Free-Speech League.

NUMBERS

The numbers one through ten are usually written out in words. Otherwise use digits.

- We have ten assignments.

- The children gathered 324 signatures for the petition.

If a number begins a sentence, always write out the number in words:

- Twenty-seven site visitors requested additional information.

Always hyphenate the numbers twenty-one to ninety-nine, even when they form part of a larger number:

- Three hundred and sixty-five days make up a year.

Write amounts of money in digits. If the amount is even, do not add zeros.

- The bill is $15.

- The bill is $15.35

POSSESSIVES

Form the possessive of a singular word by adding an apostrophe and "s."

- We found Jaden's coat.

Words of one syllable always require an added "s" to form the possessive. All singular nouns—even those that end in "s"—always take an apostrophe and "s."

- Gus's pictures were prominently displayed.

- Mr. Jones's briefcase was damaged in the fire.

- Bring the signed contract to Mavis's office.

For a plural noun that ends in "s," add only the apostrophe to form the possessive.

- The families' houses are all similar, but they all had different builders.

- The Joneses' lease ends in July.

EXAMPLES:
CIRCLE THE CORRECT ANSWER

1. The (painting's/paintings'/paintings's) tones warm up the room. (plural)

2. When (Madison's/Madisons'/Madisons's) mother shows up with the cupcakes, give me a call. (singular)

3. Did you see Julie (Andrews'/Andrews's/Andrew's) performance in the play? (singular)

4. Mr. (Coate's/Coates's/Coates') lecture on Mark (Twain's/Twains'/Twains's) novel was very insightful. (singular)

5. Do you have the Number 77 (bus's/busses'/bus')schedule? (singular)

CONTRACTIONS

Use contractions to warm up your tone. Contractions make writing more conversational. These days, contractions are usually appropriate except in legal or the most formal writing. Unless instructed otherwise, you can use contractions in academic writing.

- It's time to get ready for the annual picnic.
- Don't worry! We'll get there on time!
- Scientific studies haven't yet proven the premise.

IT'S versus ITS

It's is a contraction of the two words *it is.* You can think of the apostrophe as replacing the missing "i" in *is.*

- It's a beautiful day. (It is a beautiful day.)

Its is a possessive pronoun.

- The dog hurt its paw.

WHO vs. WHOM

After a preposition use **whom**:

- *For* Whom the Bell Tolls
- *To* Whom It May Concern

After a to-be verb use **who**:

- Shanti is who I called.
- He was the guy who won.

I vs. Me and He, or She vs. Him or Her

A simple way to decide which pronoun to use: Drop the first subject to see which pronoun sounds right. For example:

- Joe and (me/I) went to the store.

Me went to the store? No. I went to the store.

- Joe and I went to the store.

- Will you give it to her or to me/I?

Will you give it to I? No.

- Will you give it to me?

Me, Myself, and I

Do not use myself as a substitute for I or me. Use *intensive pronouns* (myself, yourself, herself, etc.) for emphasis or as a *reflexive* (never as a subject):

- Emphasis on a preceding noun or pronoun:
  She, herself, is a vegetarian.

- Reflexive pronoun:
  She gave herself a pat on the back.
  I gave myself a raise.

ABBREVIATIONS AND ACRONYMS

Abbreviations

In formal writing, abbreviations are generally not acceptable. In the body of the document, you should not abbreviate the following:

- streets

- locations

- units of measurement

- months

- state names

- titles

Abbreviations **can** be used for the following:

- footnotes

- company names

- outside addresses (on envelopes)

- a.m./p.m. or A.M./P.M. (Just be consistent.)

Acronyms and Initialization

Technically, an **acronym** is a combination of first letters of a phrase that creates a word. And **initialization** is the creation of a name using first initials, but the initials do not create a new word. For example, here are a few acronyms—initials that have become words:

- AIDS: acquired immune deficiency syndrome

- NATO: North Atlantic Treaty Organization

- Scuba: Self-Contained Underwater Breathing Apparatus

- FAQ: Frequently Asked Questions

- IRA: Individual Retirement Account

- CD-ROM: Compact Disc Read-Only Memory

- JPEG: Joint Photographic Experts Group

- MoMA: Museum of Modern Art

And here are a few initializations (also commonly called acronyms):

- CIA: Central Intelligence Agency

- FBI: Federal Bureau of Investigation

- USC: University of Southern California

The first time you use an acronym in a document, **spell out the complete name first** and enclose the acronym in parentheses. You can then use the acronym for the rest of the document.

- Total Annual Plan (TAP)

Acronyms of widely know organizations (CIA, NATO, ROTC) do not need to be spelled out.

DANGLING AND MISPLACED MODIFIERS

A dangling or misplaced modifier is usually some form of an adjective that does not correctly modify (describe) a noun. Check sentences that have two clauses **in which the first clause has no stated subject**.

The first phrase must describe (modify) the subject stated in the following clause, which will be the first noun that follows the comma.

Before:

Trained and eager for the race, Seth's chances were at an all time high.

The reader "gets it" that the writer means that Seth is the subject of the first phrase—but grammatically, the first noun that follows the comma is "chances." *Seth* functions here as an adjective describing the noun *chances.* And chances are not trained and eager for the race. Seth does not appear in this sentence as a subject at all. And this creates a dangling modifier: No one in this sentence describes who is trained and eager for the race. "Trained and eager" needs a noun to modify--to describe. WHO is trained and eager? No one. So the modifier, the opening description, dangles.

After:

Trained and eager for the race, Seth felt that his chances were at an all time high.

The first noun to follow the comma? Seth. He is the subject of the second clause—and now he is the subject of the description in the first phrase—the description of Seth. Seth is trained and eager for the race—AND—he feels his chances are at an all time high.

A misplaced modifier is a word or phrase that modifies (describes) a noun that appears in the sentence but not in the correct grammatical location.

Before:

Singing in public for the first time, stage fright overwhelmed Elvis, and he dropped his guitar.

This sentence is incorrect because the introductory phrase "Singing in public for the first time" should describe Elvis, but instead it modifies "stage fright"—the first noun to follow the comma.

157

After:

Singing in public for the first time, Elvis was overwhelmed with stage fright and dropped his guitar.

EXAMPLES:
REWRITE THE FOLLOWING SENTENCES TO CORRECT THE DANGLING AND MISPLACED MODIFIERS

1. Running behind, the dinner reservations were for 7:30, and Brian wouldn't make it to the restaurant until 8:15.
After:

2. Bored with the long-winded presentation, the ice cream was melting and the guests only wanted to get their dessert.
After:

3. Reading the exam over one last time, the clock ran out before Contessa could correct her mistakes.
After:

4. Waving from the platform, the train pulled out as the soldier caught a last glimpse of his new bride.
After:

5. Furious at the bad customer service, the operator hung up on Barney before he could tell her the rest of the phone number.
After:

6. Upon leaving the theater, a poster in the lobby inspired the couple to go right back inside to see another movie.
After:

7. Wanting to impress his parents, the new car in the driveway announced Jamal's promotion.
After:

8. Blessed with good looks and a high I.Q., the job was a shoe-in.
After:

9. With a background in computer science, the résumé was sure to grab someone's attention in the department.
After:

10. Baked to perfection, you couldn't ask for a tastier piece of cake.
After:

PRONOUN REFERENCE

Watch for the following problems with pronouns:

1. Avoid shifts within the same sentence between persons and numbers.

Before:
When <u>someone</u> leaves home for the first time, <u>you</u> usually feel lonesome.

After:
When <u>someone</u> leaves home for the first time, <u>he or she</u> usually feels lonesome.
OR
When <u>you</u> leave home for the first time, <u>you</u> usually feel lonesome.
OR
When some <u>people</u> leave home for the first time, <u>they</u> usually feel lonesome.

2. Avoid using the generic "he" to describe categories of people.

Before:
If the <u>student</u> is late, <u>he</u> should check in with the T.A.
After:
If the <u>student</u> is late, <u>he or she</u> should check in with the T.A.
OR
If <u>students</u> are late, <u>they</u> should check in with the T.A.

159

3. Make sure you provide a clear antecedent.

Before:
<u>They</u> say cow's milk is actually bad for humans over the age of four years old.

After:
<u>John Robbins</u>, a nutritionist, claims that cow's milk...

EXAMPLES:
RE-WRITE THE SENTENCES TO CORRECT THE PRONOUN REFERENCE PROBLEMS

1. After the accident, the car was really badly damaged, including the CD player. No one was sure if you could fix it.
After:

2. When Sean moved into the apartment, he brought his dishes, clothes, books, and most of his brother's electronics. He put them in the upstairs room.
After:

3. If you feel unsure of what class to take first, people can sign up for academic counseling in the student center.
After:

4. If you want to put the books in the crates, just stack them up at your place until I can pick them up at the end of the semester.
After:

5. They put signs in the lobby directing everyone to fill out the housing information forms before giving them back to them.
After:

6. The police told the students that they could sell their used bikes at the end of the year.
After:

7. Sarinda asked Josie and Samantha if they wanted to join the group, but she said she was already working with someone else.
After:

8. While Isaiah Huntington McGuire III is a trust-fund baby, he hasn't really leveraged it very well.
After:

9. It makes me furious when I think about the time I spent with him last summer.
After:

10. Shannon and Brice got married on the 4th of July in bathing suits on the beach with a dog for best man and wedding vows made up from song titles. That was just ridiculous.
After:

EXAMPLES:
CIRCLE THE CORRECT ANSWER

1. The last (five, 5) assignments will be due during the final (thirty, 30) days of the course.

2. (Chris', Chris's) books are for sale, but the (librarys', library's) books are free.

3. Last weekend Rachel gave Tom and (I, me) a ride to the game.

4. The paintings in the foyer belong to the (school, School) (superintendent, Superintendent).
5. You can get a (Government, government) loan if you qualify.

6. Every (childs's, child's, childs') future depends on the quality of (his, their, his or her) education.

7. All of the team members, including Cherie and (myself, I, me) contributed to the overall success of the plan.

8. As a traveler, I always plan trips to (northern, Northern) areas during the summers.

9. (Sixteen, 16) people attended the meeting, but only (eight, 8) of them stayed until the end.

10. The (professor/Professor) should ask for (peoples's, people's, peoples') evaluations before the last day.

TRANSITIONS

WORDS THAT LINK THOUGHTS

again	besides	in addition
also	further	likewise
and	next	moreover
then	last	furthermore

WORDS THAT COMPARE IDEAS

also	likewise
similarly	in the same way

WORDS THAT CONTRAST IDEAS

however	yet	on the contrary
still	although	after all
but	despite	even though
granted		
conversely		
on the other hand		
nevertheless		

WORDS THAT SHOW SEQUENCE

after	following
last	before
next	while
during	in the first place
first	second
later	earlier

WORDS THAT SHOW CAUSE & EFFECT

due to	hence
thus	because
since	therefore (an idea)
because	consequently (an action)

WORDS THAT SUMMARIZE

finally	to sum up
in short	thus

WORDS THAT EMPHASIZE

clearly	indeed	in fact

COMMONLY MISUSED WORDS

accept (to receive)
except (but)

access (to pass)
excess (extreme)

affect (to influence)
effect (noun: result; verb: to bring about)

aggravate (to add to a troubling condition)
irritate (annoy)

all right ("agreed")
alright (incorrect)

allude (indirect reference)
elude (to evade)

altar (religious)
alter (to change)

among (more than two)
between (only two)

compliment (praise)
complement (to complete)

comprises (includes)
composes (constitutes)

disinterested (impartial)
uninterested (not interested)

illicit (illegal)
elicit (draw forth)

ensure (to make sure)
insure (to underwrite)

etc. (literally, "and other things"; not to be used at the end of a list introduced by "such as" or "for example.")

farther (a greater distance)
further ("furthermore")

imply (something suggested)
infer (something deduced)

163

can (able)
may (has permission)

irrespective (independent of)
irregardless (incorrect; should be "regardless")

loan (noun)
lend (verb)

it's (it is)
its (possessive pronoun)

less: (quantity)
fewer: (number)

thorough (complete)
through (finished)
threw (past tense of throw)

loan (noun)
lend (verb)

to (preposition)
too (also)
two (number)

stationary (not moving)
stationery (writing paper)

their (pronoun)
there (place)
they're (they are)

verbal (in writing)
oral (in speech)

your (possessive)
you're (you are)

capital (seat of government of a state or county)
capitol (building)

like (governs nouns and pronouns: "Anita looks like her mother.")
as (used before clauses and phrases; Anita studies hard, as a college student should.")

shall (expresses belief. "I shall go broke if no one lends me money!" First person only)

unique (without equal; no degrees of uniqueness such as "most" or "very")

will (expresses determinarion or consent; "John will go to Texas tno matter what!" Second and third person.)

EXAMPLES:
CIRCLE THE CORRECT WORD IN THE FOLLOWING SENTENCES

1. Raquel asked her mother to (loan, lend) her $25.

2. Don't go any (farther, further) in the text until you get instructions.

3. Do you think we (can, may) eat in the cafeteria after 9:00 p.m.?

4. Todd, Albert, and Nick constantly argue (among, between) themselves.

5. You should contribute ideas to the meeting (irrespective, irregardless) of your personal feelings about Gayani.

6. The new team (composes, comprises) Adrian, David, and Harold.

7. If you have (less, fewer) items than the person in front of you, you can ask to move forward.

8. Every time we talk about literature, Elia (eludes, alludes) to his father's published poems.

9. When you have time, you should stop by his office on the third floor of the (capital, capitol).

10. The software package (compliments, complements) the rest of the platform.

TITLES

All words in a title should be capitalized except short prepositions and articles —such as, the, a, an, and, for, by, as, to, with, etc.—unless the article is the first word in the title. Some publications have dispensed with this rule, but you will always be correct if you follow it. And you could be wrong if you don't.

Who's Afraid of Virginia Woolf?

The New Hampshire Gazette

"Girls Just Want to Have Fun"

Caps or Quotation Marks?

Ask Yourself: Big (or long) or Small (or short)?

BIG/LONG: Italicize (what used to be underlined prior to personal computers— an instruction to a printer to italicize the title, which typewriters couldn't do)

small/short: quotation marks

BIG/LONG:

- BOOKS
- PLAYS
- OPERAS
- WHOLE CDS (ALBUMS)
- ANTHOLOGIES
- NEWSPAPER NAME
- MOVIES
- TELEVISION SERIES OR PROGRAMS

small/short:

- CHAPTERS
- SCENES/ACTS
- SONGS/TRACKS
- SHORT STORIES
- ARTICLES AND ESSAYS
- TELEVISION EPISODES WITHIN A SERIES
- POEMS

EXAMPLES:

1. Have you read William Faulkner's novel *The Sound and the Fury*?

2. *The Boston Globe* ran an article in December called "Where is Santa When You Need Him?"

3. Last season's episode titled "The Purple Lady" from the program *How Do I Look?* was nominated for an Emmy.

4. I love the song "White Flag" from Dido's CD *Life for Rent*.

5. You should buy *The Norton Anthology of Poetry* if you want a good critique of the poem "The Raven" by Edgar Allen Poe.

6. The famous "Hold the Mayo" scene from the movie *Five Easy Pieces* remains an all-time classic.

7. We have to write a report on George Orwell's essay "Shooting an Elephant" for our English class.

8. I wonder if George Orwell knew that his novel *1984* would become a classic.

9. Did you ever see the episode "The Soup Nazi" from the old *Seinfeld* series?

10. I wrote a term paper on the chapter "Deepening Our Connection to Others" from the book *The Art of Happiness* by His Holiness the Dalai Lama.

EXAMPLES:
UNDERLINE (TO SHOW THE TITLE SHOULD BE ITALICIZED) OR ENCLOSE IN QUOTATION MARKS THE FOLLOWING TITLES. CORRECT ANY CAPITALIZATION PROBLEMS.

1. I didn't understand the chapter the Whiteness of The Whale in Melville's novel Moby Dick.

2. In my opinion, the movie Shrek 3 was better than the first two shrek movies.

3. Whenever I plan to ski, I make sure I read the chapter Awareness increases control in the book Inner skiing.

4. Miles Davis's album Kind OF Blue sets the bar for great trumpeters, especially the cut So What.

5. If you get a chance, you should read David Sedaris's book When You are engulfed in Flames. You'll love it.

6. When I read Eckhart Tolle's book The Power Of now, I focused mostly on the chapter Dissolving Unconsciousness.

7. The Orange County Register reported a story about Police Investigations in an article called Who, what, when, and Where Were you on the Night Of The Crime?

8. The movie Miami Vice was a takeoff on the old television series also called Miami Vice.

9. PBS aired the program murder on the Orient Express as part of its series Mystery!

10. The Yellow Boat is on the list of short stories we can read from the Collected works of Stephen Crane.

checklist

Before you turn in your final draft, ask yourself if you've done the following:

1. Read your draft aloud--preferably to someone else?

2. Opened with a hook?

3. Eliminated every unnecessary word?

4. Circled all to-be verbs and replaced them with active verbs?

5. Used passive voice only for good reason?

6. Made sure every pronoun refers to its closest antecedent?

7. Wrote it the way you would say it?

8. Kept your main idea (actor/action/direct object) intact in every sentence?

9. Proofed ONE MORE TIME to make sure you've followed the Four Must-Know Rules of Punctuation?

10. Nailed the ending?

LET YOUR IDEAS BE COMPLEX.

KEEP YOUR WRITING SIMPLE.

EASY READING

IS DAMN HARD WRITING.

You've got to be a good date for the reader.

Kurt Vonnegut

The All-Nighter Writer

Marilyn Jones, PhD has logged thousands of hours as a professional writer and editor. She taught English and composition at the college level for more than 10 years. She has also taught business writing seminars in both the public and private sectors. She knows first-hand why most writing textbooks don't work.

So she wrote a book that does work.

www.allnighterwriter.com

CPSIA information can be obtained
at www.ICGtesting.com
Printed in the USA
R6609800001B